1967

Intimate Notebook, 1840-1841

Gustave Flaubert

Intimate Notebook
1840-1841

INTRODUCTION, TRANSLATION, AND NOTES
BY

FRANCIS STEEGMULLER

Doubleday & Company, Inc.
Garden City, New York
1967

Intimate Notebook, 1840–1841 was first published in France, in 1965, by Buchet/Chastel, under the title *Souvenirs, notes, et pensées intimes* with an Introduction by Lucie Chevalley Sabatier

Introduction

Introduction

This early *Intimate Notebook* of Flaubert's was recently published in France,* and parts of the present introduction to this translation into English will consist of extracts from the charming *avant-propos* written by Lucie Chevalley Sabatier to explain to French readers the provenance of the text.

A prominent character in the life story of Gustave Flaubert is his niece Caroline, to whom so many of his letters are addressed. She was the third Caroline in the family, that being the name also of her mother (Flaubert's sister) and of her maternal grandmother. The middle Caroline married, to Flaubert's dismay, an unstable but apparently otherwise undistinguished young man named Emile Hamard. Within a year of the marriage she had given birth to the third Caroline, and a few months later was dead of puerperal fever. The baby's grieving grandmother (herself a recent widow, her husband, Dr. Achille-Cléophas Flaubert, having died shortly before the baby's birth) and her Uncle Gustave took her to their country house at Croisset, outside Rouen. There she was brought up, her father be-

* Gustave Flaubert, *Souvenirs, notes, et pensées intimes*. Avant-propos de Lucie Chevalley Sabatier. Paris, Buchet/Chastel, 1965.

ing chiefly absent and gradually drifting into a life of al-
coholism and eventual madness. The girl had an English
governess and followed courses devised by Flaubert himself; she grew up to be an intellectual young woman, in-
terested in art and literature, philosophy and theology.

When it came time for this third Caroline to marry,
there were, perhaps among others, two candidates for her
hand. One was a young doctor named Franklin Grout.
He was the son of a colleague of Dr. Flaubert's, Dr. Par-
fait Grout, whose admiration for Benjamin Franklin was
such that he named his first son (who died in infancy)
Franklin, named his daughter Frankline (Frankline became a school friend of the middle Caroline), and named
his second son again Franklin. Franklin Grout was an intellectual young man, who seems to have been forced into
the study of medicine by his father, disliked it, and became a psychiatrist. But Franklin Grout was not well off,
and his suit was discouraged—according to family tradition,
by Flaubert himself. In any case, when a more prosperous
suitor came forward, Ernest Commanville, a lumber merchant, and Caroline, apparently finding Commanville
rather dull, wrote her uncle for advice, he replied:
"Mon Bibi, . . . Wit and delightfulness are qualities found
almost exclusively among people who live bohemianly.
Now the thought of my dear niece being married to a
poor man is so atrocious that I cannot entertain it for a
moment. Yes, *ma chérie,* I swear I'd rather you married a
millionaire grocer than a poverty-stricken great man. . . .
You will have a hard time finding a husband who is your
superior in mind and education . . . so you are obliged
to take somebody good but inferior. But will you be able

to love a man whom you will always have to consider from your higher level?"

Caroline married her lumber merchant and didn't have too good a time of it. He failed in business (Flaubert's capital went to pay some of the debts); when he was afloat again she pursued her intellectual interests on her "higher plane," and when he suddenly died it was in the house of another, consolatory lady, whose existence Caroline had not suspected.

Meanwhile Mademoiselle Frankline Grout, her mother's school friend, had met and married a well-known Protestant theologian, the Reverend Auguste Sabatier, and had several children, and it was in this household that Caroline sought shelter after the shock of her husband's death and its revelations. Dr. Franklin Grout had never married; he was a psychiatrist in the sanitarium of the famous Dr. Blanche in Passy; it was he who brought the raving Guy de Maupassant from the Riviera to Passy for his final incarceration. Now, in the home of his sister, Madame Sabatier, Dr. Grout found once again, free again, the Caroline he had wooed in his youth. After more time had passed, in 1900, when she was fifty-four and he fifty-seven and on the eve of retirement, they married.

This marriage, according to Lucie Chevalley Sabatier (one of the daughters of Frankline Grout and the Reverend Sabatier), was "completely happy, and gave them twenty years of cloudless companionship at Antibes, in their Villa Tanit. My uncle died in 1921, my aunt in 1931."

There is a well-known essay by Willa Cather that describes her meeting, at Aix-les-Bains about 1930, with an imposing, distinguished elderly lady who proved, to Miss Cather's delight, to be none other than this niece of the great Flaubert, his heir and literary executrix.

It was from the Villa Tanit, named for the Carthaginian goddess so prominent in *Salammbô*, that Flaubert's early *Intimate Notebook* was first sent out into the world.

"During my annual visits to my aunt, Madame Franklin Grout, at Antibes," writes Madame Lucie Chevalley Sabatier in her *avant-propos* to the French edition, "I was often asked by her to copy various manuscript pages, various letters and documents concerning her uncle Gustave Flaubert. At that time she had already written her will leaving Flaubert's chief manuscripts to libraries—the Municipal Library in Rouen, the Bibliothèque Nationale, the libraries of the Institut de France and the Musée Carnavalet—but knowing that those would be available only to specialists, she wanted the less important documents to be distributed among a larger public. The inclusion of these pieces in auction sales from time to time, she felt, would keep the great writer's memory alive.

"It may seem surprising that Madame Franklin Grout, who was responsible for the first publication of Flaubert's correspondence and the reissue of his principal works, did not see fit to publish these lesser documents herself. The fact was that she attached no importance to the increasing research being made into the youth of great writers —Stendhal, Balzac, Rimbaud; she did not foresee the interest that literary scholars and psychologists would take in the earliest efforts of such geniuses; quite the reverse—

she considered that the publication of her uncle's minor works would tend to lower rather than enhance his reputation. It was only quite late, in 1895, that she authorized the publication of certain youthful works like *Smarh* and *Novembre.*

"Recently," Madame Chevalley Sabatier continues, "when I read Professor Jean Bruneau's remarkable thesis on Flaubert's literary beginnings,* my attention was drawn to his mention of an 'intimate notebook,' which had never been published and which had apparently vanished without leaving a trace. 'This intimate notebook,' he writes, 'consists of a manuscript of sixty-five pages, entitled by Madame Franklin Grout *Souvenirs, notes, et pensées intimes,* which has never been published and which is known to us only through two sources: the extracts contained in the catalogue of the auction sale of items from the estate of Madame Franklin Grout held at the Hôtel Drouot in Paris, 18 and 19 November 1931, and the much more extensive extracts published in *Le Figaro,* 7 November 1931.'

"Despite serious attempts to trace it, the manuscript has never been found, but looking through the copies of various documents made by me years before, I found the complete text of the notebook. This I am publishing, following the advice of Professor Bruneau."

When the present translation into English was decided upon, a further search was made for the missing manuscript, but it was not found. The translation has therefore

* Jean Bruneau, *Les Débuts littéraires de Gustave Flaubert, 1831–1845,* Paris, Armand Colin, 1962.

been made from the printed French text and from the
only available source of that text—i.e. the transcript made
by Madame Chevalley Sabatier at the Villa Tanit, directly
on her typewriter, in the early 1930s. Madame Chevalley
Sabatier was good enough to lend the typescript for the
present purpose. Between it and the printed volume, certain minor differences exist, not all of them explicable as
printer's errors; some are undoubtedly improved conjectural readings made at the time of publication in 1965.
Many of Madame Chevalley Sabatier's readings, when
making her typescript in the 1930s, must inevitably have
been conjectural. Flaubert's handwriting, while more legible than many another, abounds in pitfalls; and, further-
more, the youth of eighteen and nineteen who was scrib-
bling this journal at odd moments for his own eyes alone
can scarcely have been overcareful of his penmanship.

If the manuscript were to be found, no doubt various
words or passages of both the French and English printed
texts could be changed for the better; but how many, and
just which ones, it is impossible to know for certain under
present circumstances. Certain obvious "corruptions" and
puzzles are indicated in the notes; also, some, but not all,
conjectural readings. In several of the latter I have prof-
ited from the knowledge and imagination of Professor Jean
Bruneau and Mr. Norbert Guterman. In general, this can
be said: almost all the present text is a translation of what
Flaubert certainly wrote; here and there, single words or
passages of what he wrote have had to be guessed at.

The manuscript was entitled *Souvenirs, notes, et pensées intimes* not by Flaubert himself, but by Madame
Franklin Grout, and in translation we have not scrupled
to replace it by the less cumbersome *Intimate Notebook*.

When the French text of this notebook was published in Paris in 1965, its character and importance were immediately grasped by scholars and other literary men in France. Little sympathy and perspicacity are required to understand why this should be so. Even were its authorship unknown, the *Notebook* would quite evidently be a precious, even though minor, illustration of the troubled spirit of a sensitive adolescent at the height of French Romanticism—an adolescent struggling with the flesh, swimming in philosophy, and trying to convince himself of his own faith in his literary vocation. The outpourings of youth are almost always touching; the confessions of any young person reflecting the characteristics of a clearly marked historical period are of interest to scholars; visions of literary fame and the longing to merit it by the writing of great works render any document that expresses them the opposite of trivial to artists.

This particular adolescent went on to write a number of great novels, including one often thought to be the greatest of all novels, and to express, in hundreds of superlative letters, his thoughts and feelings on art and literary creation that have inspired and otherwise engrossed several generations of readers. A record of the "humble beginnings" of such an artist and commentator on art is inevitably treasure, not trivia.

What makes a youthful notebook particularly interesting in the case of Gustave Flaubert is the circumstance, long fascinating to those familiar with his work, but particularly emphasized by scholars in recent years, that, generally speaking, the themes of Flaubert's mature novels are themes that had already engrossed him in his youthful writings—that, more consciously and more exclusively than most novelists, he used the feelings and experiences of his early years as the basis of his creations.* This is most strikingly illustrated, perhaps, by his re-use of a title— *"L'Education sentimentale"* (which might be translated "The Education of the Feelings"). That was the title he gave to an early work, written in 1845 when he was not yet twenty-four, and which he gave again to the great novel published in 1869, when he was forty-eight. The first version was never published during his lifetime. The date of the later version made possible the presence of two elements that make all the difference—the famous scenes from the revolution of 1848, and the maturity of the novelist; but fundamentally both are the same chronicle— the amorous and idealogical vicissitudes of young men from the provinces, men like Flaubert and his friends, in the Paris of the 1840s—the Paris to which Flaubert was to go, to study law, six months after the present notebook ends.

Flaubert tells us in this *Intimate Notebook:* "Before I

---

* *E.g.* Jean Bruneau, *op. cit.*, especially pp. 552–53: "To no author better than to Flaubert can we apply the words of Chateaubriand: 'The finest things that an author can put into a book are the feelings that come down to him, through memory, from the first days of his youth.' Indeed, Flaubert seems to have utilized, in his great novels, very few memories dating from later than 1843–45. At that time he stopped leading his own life in order to use his past to nourish his characters."

Jean Bruneau refers here to Flaubert's abandonment of his law studies in 1844 because of epileptic or pseudo-epileptic seizures, and his definitive retirement to his family's country house at Croisset in 1846 following the sudden deaths of his father and sister.

See also Sergio Cigada, "Genesi e struttura tematica di Emma Bovary" (*Pubblicazioni dell' Università Cattolica del Sacro Cuore, nuova serie, vol. LXXII.* N.d. [Milan, 1959], pp. 185–277).

was ten I had already begun to write"; "I began to compose as soon as I knew how to write." Many of his early stories and essays of the 1830s have been preserved and printed. Some were written at home (a wing of the Rouen hospital, where his father was chief surgeon), others as compositions for school (the Collège Royal de Rouen). All reflect the Romanticism of the age; they are heroic, or mock-heroic, or ironic—ironic especially about the bourgeoisie. Gradually the writing becomes more controlled, though remaining for the most part high-keyed and Romantic. Then, in 1842, instead of studying law with any seriousness, Flaubert completed *Novembre,* his best work so far, a well-sustained, if excessively Romantic, short novel in Chateaubriand-like prose. In the introduction to a recently reissued English translation of *Novembre,** I remarked that "It is in *November* . . . that *Madame Bovary* is most clearly foreshadowed. Many are the scenes, the descriptions, the portrayals of human traits, the epithets, that are re-used in the later, greater novel. A copy of *Madame Bovary* in which reminders of *November* were printed in a type different from the rest of the text would be a strange, patchwork sight." The present *Intimate Notebook* provides us with another link in the chain. A copy of *November,* too, in which reminders of the *Intimate Notebook* were printed in a type different from the rest of the text, would reveal the same patchwork pattern.

In the reminiscence of the Michaelmas ball at the château of the Marquis de Pomereu (page 34 of the *Intimate Notebook*) we find Flaubert's earliest mention of that

---

* *November,* translated by Frank Jellinek, New York, Serendipity Press, 1967.

nobleman, whose ball was to inspire, years later, Emma Bovary's great night of dancing at the "Château de la Vaubyessard." Counterparts of the orgies and butcheries of Assur (pages 29–30) appear twenty-two years later, in *Salammbô*. Readers of the great travel notes and travel letters of 1849–50 will feel a shock of recognition as they read Flaubert's comments on his first "wonderful trip," the trip to the Pyrenees and Corsica in 1840 (pages 31–34). It was "wonderful" particularly because during the course of it he first experienced *volupté,* in the arms of Eulalie Foucaud de Lenglade at Marseille—an experience that inspired the central episode of *November.* Probably he had worn, that night in Marseille, the "linen suit" that he occasionally looks at with such nostalgia in his wardrobe in Rouen. The desert, too, so wildly satisfying during the 1849–50 trip to Egypt and the Near East, so prominent in *Salammbô,* makes its first appearance here (page 34), in the form of a longing.

But what one prizes most, in this *Intimate Notebook,* is the total impression—the picture of the gifted, unsure young Flaubert of eighteen and nineteen (he so longs for the future that he calls himself twenty), burning with physical desire, with desire for accomplishment and fame, pouring out his heart in notations of events, in apostrophes, in reflections, in bits of narrative invention, in self-confidence and self-doubt, in what can only be called, as a whole, a divine discontent. "Divine" because, as we now know, the young notebook writer's faith in his literary vocation—that faith that waxes and wanes from entry to entry—was nothing less than the early stirring of creation itself.

Francis Steegmuller

Intimate Notebook, 1840-1841

Votre aimable lettre fait m'a mouillé les paupières
de votre "understanding" — et d'ailleurs confirme
chez moi une théorie esthético-morale : le cœur
est inséparable de l'esprit. Ceux qui ont distingué
l'un de l'autre n'avaient ni l'un ni l'autre.

Ce billet est écrit de -2 décembre- car je ne
suis très foible et j'ai la tête vuide.
Ce qui ne m'empêche pas de vous baiser sur
les deux joues amoureusement

G. Flaubert

. . . from a letter by Flaubert to his niece Caroline, Madame
Franklin Grout, who as his heir and literary executrix preserved the
text of this early *Intimate Notebook.*

Ideas are more positive than things.

If you grant me that man has a soul, I like to think that animals have souls, too—all animals, from the pig to the ant, even the microscopic animals. If man is free, animals are free; like him they will be rewarded or punished. So many different souls, so many hells, so many heavens,[1] Voltaire would have said. This reflection is humiliating. It leads to materialism or to nihilism.

I put improvisation above reflection, feeling above reason, mercy above justice, religion above philosophy, the beautiful above the useful, poetry above all.

I expect nothing good from men. No treachery, no vileness will surprise me.

I like being angry; anger enjoys itself. I feel that I shall have a very ordinary life in the world, sensible and reasonable—that I shall be a good bootblack, a good stablehand, a good re-soler of sentences, a good lawyer—whereas I'd like to have an extraordinary life.

I like luxury and lavishness, but also simplicity; women and wine, solitude and society, seclusion and travel, winter and summer, snow and roses, calm and storm; I like to love, I like to hate. Every contradiction, every absurdity, every folly—I harbor them all.

I don't count even on myself—perhaps I shall be a vile creature, ignoble, wicked, cowardly, how can I tell? And yet I think I shall have more virtue than others because I have more pride. Therefore, praise me.

I go from hope to anxiety, from wild optimism to dreary negation; it's rain and sun, but it's a gilded cardboard sun and a nasty rain with no storm.

Oh, if I could carry all my meditations and thoughts to their conclusion, and build a monument using all my dreams as scaffolding! In short, am I to be a king, or just a pig?

Never will man know the Cause, for the Cause is God; he knows only[2] successions of phantom Forms; a Phantom himself, he runs among them, tries to catch them, they flee; he runs after them, back and forth, stops only when he falls into the absolute void, then he rests.

Miracle, in religion, is an absurdity—it has importance only in the brains of philosophers.

I hear people say: no religion, but morality; that is to say, there is neither reward nor punishment, neither good nor bad, nothing comes after the human carcass and the oaken casket—be virtuous, suffer—humiliate yourselves, make sacrifices—be vicious, kill, pillage—you will be neither more nor less happy in eternity.

If time is less in eternity than the jump of a flea in time, and if you think of fame, and of the joy of living first on earth and then in the memory of men . . .

Art is more useful than industry, the beautiful more useful than the good; were it otherwise, why wouldn't the earliest nations and their rulers have been concerned primarily with industry and trade? They were artists, poets, they built useless things like pyramids, cathedrals; they produced poems before cloth—the spirit is greedier than the stomach.

I want Jesus Christ to have existed,[3] I am sure that he did—why? Because I find the mystery of the passion the most beautiful thing in the world.

Philosophy: a new science, which speaks neither to the heart nor to the senses, for there are only two things, poetry or beauty, and the useful or profitable; if you want to be a God, be a poet; if you want to be . . .

There are two kinds of vanity: public vanity, and private vanity which is called good conscience, human respect, self-esteem, so true is it that there are in each man two men, he who acts and he who criticizes. Inner life is the perpetual wheedling, by the man who acts, of the man who criticizes. If you refrain from doing something vile, if you show overconsideration in something, do you know why? It is to be able to tell yourself, as you look into your mirror, "This is the man, the wonderful man, who did that." How many women there are who blush at compliments made to them by others, but make themselves yet more extravagant compliments in private. How many poets who bow low before others, yet stand up tall when they are alone, and discover genius in their own eyes, their own heads! How many people dress for their own self-admiration, smile to see themselves smile—speak in order to marvel at their own words—practice virtue for the sake of self-esteem! Have you never been childish enough to practice attitudes that were becoming to you, sufficiently en-

amored of yourself to kiss your own hand, just to see what
it feels like?

I can talk about pride as an expert, and I shall write a
fine chapter about it some day.

I sometimes experience historical revelations, so clearly
do certain things come back to me—perhaps metempsy-
chosis really exists—sometimes I think I have lived at different epochs; indeed I have memories of them.

I have loved only one man as a friend, and only one
other, my father.[4]

After a ball, after a concert or any large gathering,
when one is once more alone one feels an immense boredom and an indefinable melancholy.

The XVIIIth century understood nothing about poetry,
nothing about the human heart; it understood everything
having to do with intelligence.

Between artist and poet, an immense difference; one
feels and the other speaks; one is the heart and the other
the head.

The political future is a machine, or, on the contrary, perhaps, we may be on the eve of an era of barbarism. I wouldn't mind a bit seeing all civilization crumble like a mason's scaffolding before the building was finished—too bad! The philosophy of history would have to be rewritten.

I'd enjoy being at the gates of Paris with five hundred thousand barbarians, and burning the whole city. What flames! What a ruin of ruins!

I have no love for the proletariat, and I do not sympathize with its wretchedness, but I do understand and share its hatred of the rich man.

Wealth brings but one advantage—a life without money worries.

The secret of being happy consists of knowing how to enjoy yourself—enjoy being at table, in bed, enjoy standing up, sitting down, enjoy the nearest ray of sunshine, the slightest bit of landscape: in other words, love everything. Thus it follows that to be happy you must already be so—there's no bread without leavening.

Stoicism, the sublimest kind of stupidity.

Modesty, the proudest kind of groveling.

There is something superior to reasoning—improvisation; there is something that judges better than judgment—tact, which is simply an inspired way of dealing with things, of behaving in the world.

There is something subtler than taste. It is not enough to have a taste for something. You must have the palate for it. Boileau certainly had taste, a fine, delicate, Attic taste; he was a little gourmet of poetry, with the daintiness of a pretty woman. But Racine had a poetic palate; he apprehended the flavor of poetry, its flower, its amber perfume, the purest essence of that mysterious thing which charms, excites, makes you smile. This sense, for those who have it, is more infallible than one-and-one-makes-two.

Friday, 28 February 1840

I just read over this notebook and pitied myself.

What is the matter with me today? Is it satiety, is it desire, disillusion, dreams of the future? My head aches, my heart is empty; ordinarily I have what is called a gay nature, but there are voids there, frightful voids into which I fall, crushed, battered, annihilated!

I no longer write—formerly I wrote, I was enthusiastic about my ideas, I knew what it was to be a poet, I was one, inside at least, in my soul, as all the generous-hearted are. The form was always faulty, it expressed my thought badly —but no matter—I was a sublime musician playing on a rebec; I was conscious of bursts of brilliance and of suave passages like noiseless kisses, silent whispers. If I had had a fine voice, how I would have sung! People would have laughed at me had they known how I was admiring myself, and they would have been right; all my accomplishment remained within me; I never wrote a line of the beautiful poem in which I took such delight. I remember that before I was ten I had already begun to write—I dreamed of the splendors of genius, a lighted hall, applause, wreathes—and now, although I am still convinced of my vocation, or else am full of immense vanity, I doubt more and more. If you knew what anguish that is! If you knew what my vanity is—what a savage vulture, how it eats my heart—how alone I am, isolated, suspicious, low, jealous, selfish, ferocious! Oh, the future I dreamed of— how marvelous it was! Oh, the life I used to build for myself, like a novel: what a life! How hard it is for me to renounce it!—and love, too, love!—I used to tell myself that when I was twenty someone would certainly love me, that I would meet someone, no matter whom, some woman, and I would know what it is, that beautiful word that was setting all the fibers of my heart, all the muscles of my flesh, aquiver with anticipation.

However, I fell in love like anybody else and no one knew anything about it. What a pity! How happy I might have been. I often find myself thinking of that, and scenes unfold amorously as in a dream. I imagine long embraces —sweet words that I repeat to myself, caress myself with —intoxicating glances. Ah, if you have had in your life something more than the caresses of whores, something more than glances that were sold, have pity on me.

Love, genius—that was the heaven that I felt, that I caught glimpses of, whose emanations came to me—visions that drove me insane; and then it closed over forever—so who will have me? It should have happened already; I have such need of a mistress, of an angel![5]

People tell me I am conceited—but then why this doubt that I have about everything I do, this void that frightens me, all these lost illusions?

Oh, a woman, what a wonderful thing! Add two wings and you have an angel! I love to dream of her contours. I love to dream of the charm of her smiles, of the softness of her white arms, the shape of her thighs, her attitude as she bends her head.

Often I am in India, in the shade of banana trees, sitting on mats; bayaderes are dancing, swans are fluffing out their feathers on blue lakes, nature throbs with love.

A week ago I thought for two hours about a pair of dainty green shoes and a black dress; not to mention the other foolish things that keep my heart occupied for long periods—I toy with absurd notions, tickle myself to make myself laugh, imagine pictures for myself to look at, pictures with rosy horizons and splendid sunshine—everything in them is bliss and radiance.

Oh! The man writing this is the same man who might have been a genius, who might have made a name for himself in the future. Ah! How wretched I am!

I'd love to be a mystic; it must give you a wonderful feeling to believe in paradise, to drown in waves of incense, to annihilate yourself at the foot of the Cross, take refuge on the wings of the dove. There is something naïve about First Communion; let us not laugh at those who weep on that occasion; an altar covered with sweet-smelling flowers is a lovely thing. The life of a saint is glorious, I should have liked a martyr's death; and if there is a God, a good God, a God who is the father of Jesus, let him send me his grace, his spirit, I will accept it and prostrate myself. I well understand that people who fast regale themselves with their hunger and enjoy their privations; it is a much more refined sensualism than the other kind; these are pleasures, thrills, raptures of the heart.

The so-called pleasure one takes in doing a good deed is a lie; it is no different from the pleasure felt by a man who is digesting. Heroism is different. But I say that when you have given a coin to a beggar and then tell yourself that you are happy, you are an imposter; you are deceiving yourself. Every good deed is more than three-quarters pride; that leaves one quarter to account for interestedness, irresistible animal impulse, need, actual appetite.

One incomprehensible thing is the infinite. But who doubts it? So there are things beyond the reach of our intelligence and we believe that they exist. Is there perhaps something which thinks, other than this same intelligence —something which is convinced that our reason _____ [6]

Why is it that when we do not share the feelings of people we are talking with, we feel clumsy and embarrassed? I recently saw a man who told me that his brother was dying; he pressed my hand affectionately, and I simply let him press it, and as I left him I gave a stupid laugh, as I might have smiled at a party.

I was annoyed at once; that man humiliated me. He was full of a certain feeling and I was quite devoid of it. I saw him again yesterday. He is a pathetically stupid fellow,[7] but I remember how I hated myself and found myself detestable at that moment.

Sensual pleasure is pleased with itself; it relishes itself, like melancholy—both of them solitary enjoyments, all the more intense because in each case their subject is the same and their object themselves. Love, on the contrary, demands sharing. Sensual pleasure is selfish and deliberate and serious; such pleasures carried to the extreme are like orgasms of self-abuse; their self-contemplation and self-enjoyment are a kind of onanism of the heart.

There are great men whom one would have liked to see and admire; there are others with whom _____[8] vile men in History. I enjoy that, and if I were to write a book it would be on the turpitudes of great men—I am glad that great men were capable of them.

To speak to me about the dignity of the human species is a mockery; I love Montaigne and Pascal for that.

The only thing that distinguishes man from the animals is that he eats when he is not hungry, drinks when he is not thirsty—free will.

I shun discipline—mathematician's mind, narrow mind —shopkeeper's heart, dry as the wood of his counter.

"Modesty" in art is an idea that can have come only from a fool. Art in its most immodest flights is "modest" if it is beautiful, if it is great. A nude woman is not immodest; a hand that hides, a veil that covers, a fold that is made—those are immodest.

"Modesty" is a thing of the heart, not of the body; it is a varnish that glows with a velvety bloom.

There are people whose slightest gesture, whose most insignificant word, the mere sound of whose voice, disgusts and repels us.

Beauty is divine. Despite ourselves we love what is beautiful, we hate what is ugly; all dogs bark at beggars because they are ragged. Children are the same; you cannot convince them that someone they dislike, someone ugly, is good; for them this is impossible.

When artists sought to represent angels, they modeled them on female nudes.

I have already written a good deal, and perhaps I would have written well if instead of perching my feelings high in order to idealize them, and setting my thoughts up on a stage, I had let them run free in the fields, just as they are, fresh and rosy.[9]

When you write, you feel how it must be, you know that at such a spot a certain thing is needed, at another spot something else; you compose pictures for yourself that you see, you have rather the feeling that you are going to bring something to flower; you feel it in your heart like the distant echo of all the passions you are going to create; and the inability to render all that is the eternal despair of those who write; the poverty of languages, which have scarcely one word for a hundred thoughts; the weakness of man, who cannot find approximations—and to me particularly it is an eternal anguish.

Oh my God, my God, why did you cause me to be born with so much ambition? For it is certainly ambition that I have. When I was ten, I was already thinking of fame—I began to compose as soon as I knew how to write; I painted ravishing pictures for myself—I dreamed of a hall, brightly lighted and glittering with gold, of hands that were clapping, of shouts, of wreathes. They call "Author! Author!"—the author is myself, of course, he has my name, he is me, me, me; they seek me out in the corridors, in the boxes, they lean out to see me; the curtain goes up; I step forward—such ecstasy! They are looking at me, admiring me, envying me, almost loving me!

Ah! How pitiable, how pitiable to dream of it; how much more so to write it to yourself, say it to yourself. Yes, I am a great man who failed to make the grade; my kind is common today. When I consider what I have done, and all that I might have done, I tell myself that I have accomplished little, and yet what strength I have within me, if you knew all the flashes that illuminate my mind. Alas! Alas! I tell myself that at twenty I could already have created masterpieces—I have booed myself, humbled myself, downgraded myself, and I do not know even what to hope for, what I want, nor what is wrong with me—I shall never be anything but a despised scribbler, a poor conceited fool.

Oh, if I had someone to love, if there were someone who loved me! How happy I should be; glorious nights, glorious hours—some people actually do live that life! Why not me? Oh, my God, I want no other pleasures—my heart is full of sonorous chords, melodies sweeter than those of heaven: a woman's finger would make them sing, vibrate —to melt together in a kiss, in a look, am I never to know anything of all that? And yet I feel that my heart is far bigger than my head. Oh, how I would love! Come, then, come, mysterious soul, sister-soul to mine, I will kiss your footsteps; you will walk on me and I will embrace your feet and weep.

I am jealous of the life of great artists: the enjoyment of money, of art, of opulence—it is all theirs. If I could have been simply a beautiful woman dancer—or a violinist; how I should have wept, sighed, loved, sobbed.

There are sad joys and gay sadnesses.

There is a certain indefinable smile, the kind that comes to our lips when we see an object of art; the sound of a violin makes us smile; the muse within us opens her nostrils and inhales the ethereal atmosphere.

Montaigne's wit[10] is a square; Voltaire's a triangle.

Montaigne is the most delectable of all writers. His sentences have juice and meat.

When you have read the Marquis de Sade[11] and have recovered from your dazzlement, you begin to wonder whether it isn't all true, whether everything he teaches isn't the truth—and this is because you cannot resist the hypothesis of limitless mastery and magnificent power that he makes us dream of.

We are not outraged by the sight of two dogs fighting, or two children exchanging blows, or a spider eating a fly—we kill an insect without thinking. Climb a tower so high that sounds are no longer heard and men appear small; if from there you see a man kill another man you will scarcely be upset, certainly less upset than if the blood were spurting onto you. Imagine a higher tower and a greater indifference—a giant looking down on antlike creatures, a grain of sand at the base of a pyramid, and

imagine the tiny creatures slaughtering one another and
the grain of dust rising: what can any of that matter to
the giant and to the pyramid? Now you can compare nature, God, in short infinite intelligence, to that man a
hundred feet high, to that pyramid a hundred thousand.
Think, in those terms, of the insignificance of our crimes
and our virtues, of our splendors and our miseries.

A joke is the most powerful thing there is, the most
terrible; it is irresistible. There is no appeal from it, either
to reason or to feeling—a thing derided is a thing dead;
a laughing man is stronger than a suffering man. Voltaire
was the king of his century because he knew how to laugh
—his entire genius was only that; that was everything.

Gaiety is the essence of wit—a witty man is a gay man,
an ironical, skeptical man who knows life, philosophy, and
mathematics. He is reason—i.e. the power, the fatality, of
ideas. The poet is flesh and tears. The facetious man is a
burning fire.

The most immoral of all plays is *Le Misanthrope,* and
it is the finest.

Oh, flesh, flesh, that demon that keeps coming back
incessantly, that tears the book from your hands and the
cheerfulness from your heart, makes you somber, ferocious,
selfish; you repulse it, it returns; you surrender to it
ecstatically, fling yourself at it, sprawl upon it, your nos-

trils flare, your muscle stiffens, your heart palpitates—and then you fall back moist-eyed, fed up, exhausted. Such is life: a hope and a disappointment.

(Pitiable.)

The Marquis de Sade forgot two things: anthropoph-agy[12] and savage beasts—which proves that the greatest men are still small; and above all he should have made fun of vice, too; he did not, and that is his mistake.

PASTICHE[13]

It was twilight, Assur was lying on a purple bed; the perfume of flowering orange trees, the wind from the sea, a thousand dying voices reached him. And from the far end of the slaves' courtyard he heard the lions and the tigers roaring in their cages as they saw the sun setting on the mountains; they spattered their froth on the bars, and they neighed, for out there their mates were awaiting them in the glades beneath the aloes. Assur, too, neighed, and his nostrils flared in joyful anticipation of the tortures and executions to come—he rises; he walks out onto the balcony of his highest belvedere with its golden rail; he leans on it and looks out—his glance pierces the distance and swerves as an arrow is shifted along the bow before it is released;—the air is heavy, stifling, he is thirsty, he longs for blood; his balcony is decorated with heads stripped of their flesh; at night eagles and vultures swoop down and pick at the skulls; he hears the sound of their wings above his roof when the back of his concubine cracks under him and bends like an osier, when he drinks smoking blood from a white satin hand. What will he do now that he has awakened still gorged from the night's orgy? Will he give himself to his mignons, or have the Magi burn incense before him? Assur comes slowly down, and seems to feel a fairy's hand take his: she is the fairy of the joys of the triple hell that breathes the steam of battlefields and exhales a perfume of roses and human flesh; she has a spotted white gown, dotted with strong, sharp teeth, she has arms that can smother, a hand that can caress; she leads him into the galleries; lights are still burning in the crystals; the fountains are murmuring; there are corpses and _____ stretched on the floor; sighs are heard; and torn limbs knock against the ground. By his orders everything is cleared and swept, voluptuous slaves pour aromas, ravishing essences; they draw the rose-gauze curtains, set out the sofas where virile hearts grow soft and swoon beneath kisses, where breasts so marvelously swell and palpitate. Now the women are led in weeping, clad in black with roses in their hair; a secret door admits the naked mignons —Assur laughs with his eyes, kisses them, lets himself be carried in their arms—the three sisters can be heard sobbing—there is a scratching of claws on the doors—a potion drawn. . . .

Night of 2 January 1841,
written after the ball.[14]

How long ago that was written! It was a Sunday afternoon, a moment of boredom and anger; harassed as much

by the remedy as by the sickness, I put down my pen and
went out. I walked to Déville for dinner. I was on the
boulevard with Mama and we met Ballay—I was cynical
and furious!

How I have lived, since then, and how many things
took place in the interval between the last line above and
what I am writing now! Work for my examination: I
passed. I shall try to sum up those five months of life
that marked the end of what is called childhood, and the
beginning of this nameless something, the life of a man of
twenty; it is (especially for someone of my nature) neither
youth nor maturity nor decrepitude; it is all those at once;
it shares all their prominent, salient traits; even in my
calm state, my physical and moral temperament is an eclec-
ticism driven relentlessly by my fancy and the caprice of
things.

When I think back on my wonderful trip, and realize
that I am now here, I ask myself whether I am really the
same man—is it the same man who stood beside the Gulf
of Sagona that is writing here at this table on a winter
night, mild and rainy, damp and thick with mist?

Oh, Italy, Spain, Turkey. Today is Saturday—it was
also a Saturday, a certain day . . . in a bedroom like
mine, low-ceilinged, with a floor of red tiles, at this same
hour, for I have just heard it strike half past two; someone
said that time flits like a shadow. Now it is a phantom
that slips from our hands, now a specter that weighs heavy
on our breast.

I went to the ball—what is there to do at a ball? How
dreary they are, the pleasures of society, and they are even
more stupid than they are dreary. I saw young girls in
blue dresses or white dresses, their shoulders covered with

pimples, their shoulder blades protruding, with faces like rabbits, like weasels, like martens, like dogs, like cats—like imbeciles goes without saying—and all of them babbling, cackling, dancing, sweating—a lot of people emptier than the sound of a boot on the pavement were around me, and I was obliged to be their equal, uttering the same words, wearing the same clothes; they surrounded me with stupid questions, and I answered in kind. They wanted me to dance! Good little children! Sweet young things! How I longed to enjoy myself like them!

I'm foolish enough to open the wardrobe beside my bed occasionally and look at my linen suit and go through the pockets. It is we who delude ourselves, as Montaigne says.

What am I doing, what am I ever going to do, what is my future? Not that that is important. I wanted to work this year, but I haven't had the heart for it, and I am much put out about it; I could have known Latin, Greek, English; a thousand things snatch the book from my hands, and I lose myself in reveries longer than the longest hours of twilight.

I should like to know just what the impulse is that prompts me to write these pages, this one especially, to-night's pages that I mean no one to read.

Since I have put aside old Moutna, I am going to set down here in outline everything I don't want to forget.

I was given my bachelor's degree one Monday morning —I no longer remember the date—Café Duprat. Home, N____ was lunching there. I drop onto my bed and sleep, a bath that evening, take it easy for several days. I am to go to Spain with M. Cloquet. I read as much as I can about Spain; change—it is to be Corsica—I leave Rouen by the steamer—Maxime, Ernest, Huet, railroad—to Paris;

at the entrance of the Palais-Royal I run into a whore from the rue de la Cigogne, Lise. Visit to Gourgaud, we walk around the Swiss Lake, I tell him my doubts about my literary vocation, he comforts me—fine weather—same day, dinner at Vasse's.

Departure for Bordeaux—an accident to the coach, our traveling companions are a young man with glasses, wearing a black cap—discussion on a point of philosophy of history; beyond Angoulême the blue overcoat, and a little man returning from his home town, he had been in the Indies, he had been in New Zealand.

Bordeaux—theatre, a rehearsal, our hostess—dinner at General Carbonel's.

Departure for Bayonne, a thin woman and a fat woman, conductor, traveling salesman, I buy a pack of cigars.

At Bayonne—his friend the tall fellow in a gray overcoat trimmed in black, a Doctor M____ who sounds like a moralistic farmer: "I practice medicine out of philanthropy."

We go through Fuenterrabia—a boy who drives us there; yellow face of the official at the entrance to the bridge over the Bidassoa—at the inn where we eat at Behobia, Spanish girl with a striking expression of great kindness; sick to my stomach—storm that evening.

From Bayonne to Pau, Basques jammed under the tarpaulin who sang all night; officers, one of whom sitting with his back to me turns around and talks to me about literature, Chateaubriand. My neighbor on the left, yellow sandals, his hat bothers him, he puts his red handkerchief around his head, velvet overcoat, pointed snub nose.

At Pau I am cold—I read my notes to M. Cloquet and

Mlle. Lise, little praise and little intelligence forthcoming from them; I am annoyed; that night I write Mama, I feel sad; at table I can hardly restrain my tears.

This night that I am spending this way—I don't quite know why—reminds me of another, similar night; it was at the château of the Marquis de Pomereu one Michaelmas; it was during the vacation after my fifth or sixth year at school; I stayed up all night watching the dancing, and when everyone retired I threw myself on my bed, the candle was burning, and my head ached just as it does now— come, come, strong man, buck up—can't you go one night without sleep? When morning came I went rowing on the pond.

In a few minutes it will be four o'clock if the cock has crowed as in *Hamlet*—it seems to me a week already, whereas actually it is scarcely three hours, since I was watching all those people leave and the dancing end.

Stone, grotto, Les Eaux-Bonnes, Tournay, walk in the evening, baths, the woman at the drinking fountain—farewell to another day. . . .

25 January, half past four in the afternoon, the sun is still shining, my iron sundial casts its silhouette on my window curtain.

Today my ideas about a long trip took stronger hold of me than ever. Still the Orient.[15] I was born to live there. Opening the *Itinéraire* ABC at random, I saw:

"A third (a French soldier who had remained in Egypt and become a Mameluke), a tall young man, thin and pale, had lived for a long time in the desert with the

Bedouin, and he missed that life terribly; he told me that whenever he found himself alone amid the vast stretches of sand, on camelback, he would be seized by such transports of joy that he was quite beside himself." That gave me long thoughts. The idea of it makes me wish increasingly every day that I could fall into the ecstasy of the Alexandrians—the silence of the desert, whose sounds are so sweet to its sons, frightens men who come from rainy lands, men who breathe coal smoke and live with their feet in the mud of cities. Davot confessed as much to me— several times he set out by himself and didn't dare go on. Botta, whom I saw at Rouen and who lived out there a long time, used to extol the freedom of Arabia to the Abbé Stéphany, his father's fellow townsman: "That is freedom," he used to say, "the true kind; you people don't know what it is." And what he said next made me quiver with jealousy: "They wore long silk robes, great white turbans, carried superb arms, they had a harem, slaves, thoroughbred horses."

I haven't worked this month of January; I don't know why—an inconceivable laziness—I have no bones (morally speaking); there are days when I could leap up to the clouds—days when I haven't the strength to turn the pages of a book.

People over forty, their hair a bit gray, no enthusiasm amid all the tedious clichés they smother you with, have a way of telling you: "You'll change, young man, you'll change," to such a point that there isn't a single remark about life, art, politics, history, that isn't accompanied by that refrain. I remember that M. Cloquet—a great utterer of platitudes, witty man though he is—urged me one day

to write out all my ideas in the form of aphorisms, seal
the paper, and open it in fifteen years. "You'll find another
man," he told me. Since that may be an excellent bit of
advice, I am going to follow it.

I

As for morality in general, I do not believe in it; it is a
feeling and not a necessary idea.

II

I find the idea of duty inconceivable; those who pro-
claim it would, I think, be hard put to it to reconcile it
with the idea of liberty.

III

The politics of history in its human aspects; everything
that happens must happen; this must be understood, not
deplored; there is nothing so stupid as historical hatreds.

IV

I can understand all vices, all crimes; I can understand
ferocity, stealing, etc. Only baseness revolts me. Perhaps if
I saw those other things, I would feel the same about them.

V

As for the virtue of women, I believe in it more than do certain people who are very moral and very [illegible], because I believe in woman's indifference, coldness and vanity—qualities which those gentlemen take into account not at all.

VI

I feel that deep down I am a decent man, that is, devoted, capable of great sacrifices, capable of loving strongly and of strongly hating low tricks, frauds.

Everything that is petty, narrow, hurts me. I love Nero, I am passionately against censorship.

VII

I expect every possible evil from men.

VIII

I believe that humanity has but one objective: to suffer.

IX

The history of the world is a farce.

X

Great pity for people who believe in the seriousness of life.

XI

I have never understood "modesty."

XII

Great disdain for people; and yet I feel that many of my characteristics could make them like me.

XIII

I have not the slightest yearning for political success. I would rather be applauded on the stage of a music hall than on a rostrum.

XIV

Too bad that conservatives should be so despicable and republicans so stupid.

XV

Superior to everything is—Art. A book of poetry is preferable to a railroad.

XVI

If Society continues as it is going at present, in two thousand years there won't be a blade of grass or a tree; nature will have been devoured. Take a look: the present-day world seems to me a horrible spectacle. We no longer even believe in vice. The Marquis de Sade, who is considered a monster, fell into his eternal sleep calmly, like an angel—he had a faith, he died happy—and the sages of today: how do they die?

XVII

Christianity is on its deathbed. Its recent reprieve was, I think, only a final flare-up. We defend it out of opposition to all the philanthropic and philosophical nonsense that we are fed up with, but when someone comes along and talks to us about dogma, about pure religion, we feel ourselves sons of Voltaire.

XVIII

Many things have been predicted to me: *1.* that I'll learn to dance; *2.* that I'll marry. We'll see—I don't believe it.[16]

XIX

I don't see that the emancipation of Negroes and women is such a fine thing.

XX

I am neither a materialist nor a spiritualist. If I were something, it would be rather a materialist—*spettatore*—spectator.[17]

XXI

I like the celibacy of priests—although I am no worse than anybody else, the family seems to me something rather narrow and miserable—the poetry of the fireside is shopkeepers' poetry; frankly, despite all the exaggeration of the poets, there is nothing very great in it.

XXII

I feel more attachment for my dog than for a man.

XXIII

There are days when the sight of animals fills me with tenderness.

XXIV

The presents I should most welcome now: a post chaise and freedom to travel.

XXV

In my present mood, I would not be indignant if I found my servant robbing me; I couldn't help approving of it deep-down, for I don't see anything very wrong in it.

XXVI

Nothing seems evil to me.

XXVII

There is no such thing as a true idea or a false idea. At first you adopt things quickly and enthusiastically; then you reflect, then you doubt, and that's that.

XXVIII

Nobody loves praise more than I, and praise bores me.

XXIX

I enjoy hearing a menial refer to his human dignity as having been degraded, slighted, trampled upon—not because I hate mankind, but out of antipathy for the idea of dignity.

XXX

The future of humanity, the rights of the people—so much silly nonsense.

XXXI

I believe nothing and am inclined to believe everything —except moral preaching.

XXXII

These are the truly stupid things: *1.* literary criticism, whatever it may be, good or bad; *2.* the Temperance Society; *3.* the Montyon Prize[18]; *4.* a man who vaunts the human species—a donkey eulogizing long ears.

XXXIII

Here's an idea worth proposing: melt down all the statues to make coins, use the canvas of all the pictures for clothes, heat your room with the frames.

XXXIV

Corollary of the above:
Modern stupidity and greatness are symbolized by a railroad.

XXXV

Civilization is a history of anti-poetry.

XXXVI

I often wish I could cut off the heads of people on the street whose faces I don't like. (I will finish these maxims some other day.)

Resumed 8 February

I have an intermittent moral sickness: yesterday I had superb projects for work, today I cannot go on with it. I have read five pages of English without understanding it; that is nearly all that I have done, and I have written a love letter—just for the sake of writing, not because I love anyone.[19] Still, I should like to make myself believe that I do—and I do love and do believe while I am writing. For a few days I had the firm resolution to see to it that at the end of six months, about July, I should know English and Latin, and that I should be able to read Greek by the end of this week. I was supposed to memorize the fourth book of the Aeneid. I don't read very much. I would have to attach myself[20] more profoundly than I do to everything around me, to my family, to the study of the world, to everything I avoid and which—I don't know why—I want to force myself not to like (the word "world" is excessive here). I blow hot and cold about them, but only in my heart. There are days when I long to be brilliant in drawing rooms, to hear my name proclaimed admiringly; and other times I want to demean myself, lower myself, be a notary in some hole in Brittany. Chéruel[21] noticed my strange state of mind, but there is also a little affectation in the way I go on; I am always acting out a comedy or a tragedy, I am so difficult to know that I don't even know myself.

What's the use of writing this? I really couldn't say. Adieu, Gustave—see you some other day; whatever happens, there will be others spent in the _____.[22]

If you begin your book telling yourself: it must prove this or that, the reader must come away from it religious, or ungodly, or erotic—you will write a bad book, because in composing it you have offended against truth, distorted the facts. Ideas flow spontaneously, following an inevitable, natural course. If, for any purpose whatever, you try to make them take a direction that isn't their own, everything is wrong. You must let characters limn themselves according to their own logic; action must develop of itself. Everything must grow freely, and you must do no forcing in one direction or another. Examples: *Les Martyrs, Gil Blas,* Béranger.

Today, 21 May, a cold rainless day; it looks like snow, and the trees are in leaf—a day of low spirits and anxiety —such a need to write, to unbosom myself, and I don't know what to write or what to think. So it is always with confused instincts; I am a mute who wants to talk. Ah! my pride, my pride, no one realizes the extent of it, neither my family nor my friends nor myself. —After all, perhaps I am mistaken in ascribing everything to it. As I write this page I feel that I am not saying what I want to say, I

haven't found the proper outlet for my thoughts. I am
now in a strange position, just finished school and about
to go out into what is called the world. All the memories
of my past life come back to me, and I relive my eight
years of school. But it seems to me like twenty years ago
that I first entered the building one afternoon at three
o'clock, wearing a blue jacket. It was a period of inconceivable boredom and stupid dreariness, punctuated by
spasms of buffoonery. I will write that story someday, for
I yearn to tell myself about myself—everything I do, I do
to please myself. If I write something, it is to be able to
read myself; if I dress, it is to look well in my own eyes; I
smile at myself in the mirror to be amiable to myself. Such
is the motive of all my actions; have I a better friend
than myself? If I judge myself favorably, I also judge myself
pitilessly, for there are days when I aspire to the reputation
of the obscurest vaudevillian; I exalt myself and I humble
myself, so that I am never at my true level. Lately I reread
Werther; my disillusion with it was complete; everything
that had seemed warm to me in it is cold, everything that
seemed good is detestable. The future enchants me, the
present counts for little, the past reduces me to despair,
and I am not gaining in experience. I love thinking about
the future, I have always thought about it, and never has
there come to pass a single thing that I had hoped for,
expected, feared, etc.

Strength is something you enjoy as you lose it.

When I began this I wanted to make it a faithful copy
of what I thought and felt, and that didn't happen a

single time, so greatly does man lie to himself. When you look at yourself in the mirror your face is reversed; it is quite simply impossible to speak truthfully when you write something. You arouse your own feelings, you laugh at yourself, smirk at yourself; sometimes you have opposing thoughts during the writing of a single sentence. Hurry, and you spoil everything; hold yourself back, and you over-complicate and go slack.

Melancholy is a sensual pleasure that is deliberately provoked. How many people shut themselves away to make themselves sadder, or to weep beside a stream, or choose a sentimental book! We are constantly building and un-building ourselves.

There are days when one would like to be an athlete, and others when one longs to be a woman.[23] In the first case it is because your muscles are aquiver; in the second, because your flesh is yearning and ablaze.

What I lack above all is taste; I mean everything. I grasp and feel things en bloc, synthetically, without no-ticing details. I like *tutti*, the full orchestra; anything that looms up or stands out I perceive; otherwise, not. Texture and inner structure escape me; my hands are horny, and I have no real feeling for softness of material, but am at once aware of shine—half tones are not for me—this is why I love spicy things, peppery, sugary things, and things that melt in the mouth; but nothing subtle. Color, image, above all; I lack _____ and, still more, precision;—no unity; movement, but no _____. Invention, but not the slightest sense of rhythm,[24] that is what I lack most—and especially a long-winded, pretentious style.

Dramatic art is geometry expressed in music—the sublime in Corneille and in Shakespeare suggests to me a rectangle—their ideas end in right angles.

One would like to have lived like Caesar, Montaigne, Molière, Rousseau.

The sciences proceed by analysis—they think that this is their glory, whereas it is their weakness. Nature is a synthesis, and to study it you cut, you separate, you dissect, and when out of all these parts you seek to make a whole—the whole is artificial—you make the synthesis after deflowering it—the connections no longer exist—yours are imaginary, I go so far as to say hypothetical—and natural science, the science of relations between things, the science of cause and effect, the science of motion, of embryology, of articulation. . . .

I do have some tender amorous desires, but I have others that are ardent, bloody, horrible.

The most virtuous of men has horrible things in his heart.

There are thoughts and actions that you admit to no one, not even to your usual confidant, not even to your friend, that you never say aloud even to yourself.

Have you sometimes blushed at the secret, ignoble impulses that surge up in you and then die down, leaving you astonished, surprised at having had them?

I am writing these pages in order to reread them in a year, in thirty years[25]—that will take me back to my youth, like a landscape you want to see again and go back to—you remembered it as lovely, smiling, the leaves all green; not at all—it is dry, barren, no sap in the trees. Oh, I thought it was prettier, you say. I write because I enjoy it.

Thought is the greatest of pleasures—pleasure itself is only imagination—have you ever enjoyed anything more than your dreams?

A useful man. Be a chemist, a mechanic, a bootblack. They achieve results, and that is what the majority wants. Philosophy gives no results—it is all thought—poetry on the contrary is all action, images of actions or of feelings— poetry is a world—it has its seas, its streams to quench our thirst—philosophy is parched with the dust of the nothingness of all its systems.

To tell me that a priest is not useful, that a poet is not useful, and that an astronomer is more so, is to ____.

Perhaps there will come a fine day when all modern science will collapse and we'll be laughed at—I hope so.

I love to see humanity humbled. That spectacle cheers me when I am tired.

There is a rather stupid axiom which says that the word renders the thought—it would be more truthful to say that it distorts it. Do you ever utter a sentence just as you think it? Will you write a novel as you have conceived it?

If sentences really rendered thoughts! —What effect would be produced on you by pictures if you saw them as a sequence of brush strokes? I could sing you vague, delightful tunes that I have in my head and make you feel the passions that I think of; [but] I could tell you all my reveries, and you will know nothing about them—because there are no words to express them. Art is nothing but this strange translation of thought by form.[26]

Notes

As the *Intimate Notebook* opens, sometime in 1840, Gustave Flaubert, eighteen years old, is living at home with his parents and his sister Caroline in a wing of the Hôtel-Dieu, the municipal hospital of Rouen, of which his father, Dr. Achille-Cléophas Flaubert, is head. Gustave's elder brother, also named Achille, is a young doctor in Paris, soon to return to Rouen, where he will eventually succeed his father. Until the previous December, Gustave had been attending classes at the *lycée*, the Collège Royal de Rouen, where he had reached his last year, the *année de Philosophie*. In December 1839, however, he participated in a student revolt and withdrew from the *lycée*, apparently with his parents' consent or approval, and now he is studying at home, preparing privately for the examination which may win him his bachelor's degree, the *baccalauréat*. That would qualify him to enroll in the Law School in Paris, where his father wishes him to study. He himself views that prospect with no pleasure. He dreams, rather, of a literary career.

1. "heavens." In the typed transcript made by Madame Chevalley Sabatier and kindly loaned by her for the present translation into English, and in the published

French text printed in France from that transcript, the word here is *paroles* (words), which is unlikely. Conjectural change to *paradis*.

2. "he knows only." In the transcript and the published French text, this is *il ne naît que* (there is born only), which is unlikely. Conjectural change to *il ne connaît que*. Flaubert is studying Hegel and other idealistic philosophers.

3. "I want Jesus Christ to have existed." The religious tone of the Flaubert household was a combination of traditional French Catholicism and freethinking. Flaubert's father, Dr. Achille-Cléophas Flaubert, was an intellectual and scientist, like so many of his friends and colleagues. Gustave and his sister were both baptized, but whereas she made her First Communion, there is no record of his having done so. (Jean Bruneau, *Les Débuts littéraires de Gustave Flaubert, 1831–1845*, p. 281, n. 97.) The *Intimate Notebook* testifies several times to his early waves of religious mysticism, a subject which was always to fascinate him and which he treated with great power in various of his works. Reflection of these youthful religious feelings are found here and there in his early, very Romantic novel *Novembre,* begun while he was still writing the *Intimate Notebook.* For example:

"Brought up, like all my contemporaries, without religion, I had neither the dry satisfaction of the atheist nor the nonchalant irony of the skeptic. If I occasionally entered a church, doubtless merely to indulge a whim, it was to listen to the organ, to admire the statuettes in their niches; but dogma I did not aspire to, too well I felt myself the son of Voltaire."

"I thought how sweet it was to sing canticles kneeling at evening at the feet of a madonna in the light of candles, and to love the Virgin Mary, who appears to sailors in a corner of the sky, holding the sweet Jesus Child in her arms."

The latter is from a passage expressing a mood of pantheistic ecstasy.

4. "my father." Flaubert's love of his father is felt in the letters he wrote at the time of Dr. Flaubert's death; and the description of the great Dr. Larivière at the end of *Madame Bovary* is thought to reflect this affection and reverence. Jean Bruneau (*op. cit.,* p. 285, n. 113) urges us to set the present statement in the *Intimate Notebook* against the "tradition" that there was little sympathy between professional father and artistic younger son—a rumor perhaps begun by Flaubert's friend Maxime du Camp in his *Souvenirs littéraires,* where he reports Dr. Flaubert as falling asleep while Gustave read to him from the first *Education sentimentale.*

The "one man" whom Flaubert had, up until now, loved as a friend was Alfred Le Poittevin, whose sister was to become the mother of Guy de Maupassant. Le Poittevin's early death in 1848 is the occasion for one of Flaubert's most moving letters. Flaubert was soon to enter on another, long-enduring friendship—with Louis Bouilhet, who played such a great advisory role during the composition of *Ma-*

dame Bovary. Maxime du Camp also became a close early friend—it was with him that Flaubert traveled to Egypt and the Near East in 1849–1850—but their ways parted.

5. "I have such need of a mistress, of an angel!" It is particularly in these pages, and in other, similar pages of longing throughout the *Intimate Notebook,* that we find the mood, the rhythm, at times the very words, of many passages in the first part of the Romantic short novel *Novembre.*

6. "our reason _____" These lines are one of several possible readings of an obscurely phrased paragraph which in both French texts is incomplete. Madame Chevalley Sabatier tells us in a footnote that in the original manuscript the paragraph is cancelled with a red line and that the word *bête* (stupid) is written across it.

7. "a pathetically stupid fellow." Madame Chevalley Sabatier tells us in a footnote that Flaubert refers here to his schoolmate and future brother-in-law, Emile Hamard, father of Madame Franklin Grout.

8. "others with whom _____" Broken or corrupt texts here.

9. "fresh and rosy." There are differences between the two French texts in this paragraph. One or two words are conjectural.

10. "wit." The French is *esprit*. Since there is no context, the reader is free to substitute "spirit" if he prefers.

11. "Marquis de Sade." "Oh, my dear Ernest," the seventeen-year-old Flaubert had written to his friend Ernest Chevalier the previous July 15 (1839), during a mathematics class in the Rouen *lycée*, "about the Marquis de Sade—if you could find me a few of the novels by that worthy writer I would pay you their weight in gold. I have a biographical article about him by J[ules] Janin that has revolted me—revolted me on Janin's account, of course, for in it he does much declaiming on behalf of morals, on behalf of philanthropy, on behalf of violated virgins!" By January 1840 Flaubert is urging Chevalier to "read the Marquis de Sade, and read him to the last page of the last volume; that will complement your morals course and will give you brilliant insights into philosophy and history."

Sade's fascination for Flaubert never ceased. "Flaubert is really obsessed by Sade," Goncourt writes in his *Journal*. "He racks his brains to find sense in that madman. He makes him the incarnation of the *Antiphysis* and goes so far as to say, in splendid paradoxes, that he is the last word in Catholicism, the hatred of the body." (See Bruneau, *op. cit.*, p. 33, n. 96.)

However, the aspect of Sade by which Flaubert declares himself impressed in the present paragraph of the *Intimate Notebook*, "the hypothesis of limitless mastery and magnificent power that he makes us dream of," is close to what many modern readers relish in Sade's "philosophy"—that hypothesis, and its counterpart, the satisfaction felt by victims in surrendering all their will to their tormentors. See, for example, what is at present the latest example of "serious" French Sadic literature: *Story of O,* by "Pauline Réage."

12. "anthropophagy." Apparently, despite his advice to Ernest Chevalier, Flaubert himself had not yet read all the works of the Marquis de Sade.

13. "PASTICHE." As we learn from the next section of the *Intimate Notebook,* this bloody bit was written in Rouen on a Sunday afternoon, probably in August 1840, in a "moment of boredom and anger"; and after writing it Flaubert felt "harassed as much by the remedy as by the sickness"—as much by what he had written as by the mood that had set him to writing it. As a "pastiche" it seems to combine memories of his readings in ancient history with his more recent readings in the Marquis de Sade.

In the letter to Ernest Chevalier quoted above, written in the mathematics class the year before, Flaubert said: "I love to see men like . . . Nero, like the Marquis de Sade. When you read history . . . such figures are like the priapuses the Egyptians set beside the statues of the immortals, beside Memnon, beside the Sphinx. These monsters explain history for me; they are its complement, its apogee, its morality, its dessert; believe me, they are the great men, they are immortal, too. Nero will live as long as Vespasian, Satan as long as Jesus Christ." About that same time Flaubert wrote an historical dissertation, "Rome and the Caesars," well characterized by Jean Bruneau as

"A long description, full of admiration and horror, of the orgies of the imperial age." Flaubert was never to lose his love of reading and writing about blood and orgies. "I admire Nero," he was to write to a friend a few years later. "He is the culminating man of the antique world! Woe to him who does not tremble as he reads Suetonius! Lately I read the life of Heliogabalus in Plutarch. That man is of a beauty different from Nero's. His is more Asiatic, more feverish, more romantic, more unbridled: it is like a night-scene, delirium by torchlight!" All this was to culminate in the composition of *Salammbô*. Sainte-Beuve, in his review of that book, mentioned Flaubert's *"pointe d'imagination sadique."*

Flaubert's placing of his "pastiche" in ancient Assyria probably reflects his early acquaintance in Rouen, which we learn of from a later entry in the *Intimate Notebook*, with Paul-Emile Botta, the French consul in the Near East who in 1843 began to excavate Khorsabad, thinking it was Nineveh, and later sent Assyrian reliefs to the Louvre. It is not clear whether Flaubert's picture of the king or god Assur is based even remotely on anything beyond the mere words of Genesis 10:11—"Out of that land went forth Asshur, and builded Nineveh." At this time cuneiform records had not been deciphered, and it is not known whether Flaubert had access to non-biblical Hebrew legends.

Flaubert was at this time still far from *le mot juste,* for which he later became so famous. His lions and tigers "neigh" after their distant mates, whereas (according to the New York Zoological Society) those animals when sexually aroused utter a "low growling sound." What Assur himself was meant to sound like when he, "too, neighed," one cannot say. The description of an arrow's behavior is puzzling, as is the "spotted white gown, dotted with strong, sharp teeth." The transcript has: *elle a une robe blanche tachetée, de belles dents d'acier,* the comma after *tachetée* implying that the lady herself has "strong, sharp [steel] teeth"; the published French text places the comma, instead, after *blanche,* where I have chosen to keep it.

The following clauses, present in the transcript, were for some reason omitted from the published French text: "she leads him into the galleries"; "the fountains are murmuring; there are corpses and _____ stretched on the floor; sighs are heard; and torn limbs knock against the ground." The word left blank is, in the transcript, *vins* (wines)— scarcely possible; and much of the last of these clauses is conjectural. The very last clause of the "pastiche," "a potion drawn," is, in both the transcript and the published French text, *un breuvage extrait*—probably conjectural.

14. "after the ball." Five months have passed since the last entry, the Assyrian "pastiche," and so much has happened that Flaubert wonders whether he is "the same man." He is just back from a ball, and his sleeplessness reminds him of another sleepless night, after a ball at the château of the Marquis de Pomereu some years before. (The Marquis de Pomereu is said to have been an unreconstructed aristocrat and the greatest landed proprietor in France. It was at his château in Normandy, the Château du Héron, that the Michaelmas ball took place, on 29 September 1837. Shortly after that, Flaubert had incorporated a ball scene into a youthful horror story about

a half orangoutang, half man, "Quiquid Volueris" [As You Like It]. Apparently Dr. Flaubert and his family had been invited to the Château du Héron rather—shall we say?—exceptionally. [See Jean Bruneau, *op. cit.*, pp. 494–95 and n. 67.] Later, in describing the presence of the medical officer Charles Bovary and his wife Emma at a similarly aristocratic ball at the "Château de la Vaubyessard," Flaubert was to forget neither the condescension of the invitation nor the beauty of the ball. Until he was invited by Napoléon III and the Empress Eugénie to balls at the Tuileries and at Compiègne in the 1860s, the 1837 ball at the Château du Héron seems to have been his only experience of a *"très high-life"* affair. The Marquis de Pomereu would have considered the emperor and empress parvenus.)

Shortly after writing the Assyrian "pastiche," Flaubert had passed his examination and obtained his degree, 23 August 1840. As a reward, his family offered him a trip to the Pyrenees and Corsica. It would be his first traveling of any consequence, but he hesitated to accept because of the companions he would have: a colleague of his father's named Dr. Cloquet, and the latter's sister and a friend— Mademoiselle Lise Cloquet and the Abbé Stéphany. He did accept, and Dr. Flaubert wrote him a charming letter on his departure: "Profit from your trip, and remember your friend Montaigne, who thinks that one should travel chiefly in order to bring back the humors and customs of other lands, and to *'frotter et limer notre cervelle contre celle d'autruy.'* Watch, observe, take notes: don't travel like a grocer or a salesman."

Since the railroad under construction from Paris had

not yet reached Rouen, he took a Seine steamer probably
as far as Mantes, and the railroad the rest of the way to
the capital. In Paris he ran into a prostitute he had seen
in Rouen, and he went to Versailles where one of his
former Rouen professors, Gourgaud, now teaching there,
comforted him, as they walked around the Swiss Lake,
about some of his uncertainties. Then the party set out
for Bordeaux and points south.

Flaubert wrote an account of the expedition that has
been printed several times in France as *Voyage aux
Pyrénées et en Corse,* but never translated into English.
The style is heavy and self-conscious: it is evident that
even though he liked Dr. Cloquet he was oppressed by
the company of three elders. Indeed, when he next traveled south, five years later, once again in company, he
remembered his father's words and wrote to Alfred Le
Poittevin: "This is the second time I'm seeing the Mediter-
ranean like a grocer."

The *Voyage aux Pyrénées et en Corse* comes notably to
life at one point—the description of the brief stay in Marseille on the way to Corsica. The real reason for the enthusiasm is not recounted, but we know it. Dr. Cloquet
was invaluable in Marseille. He introduced Flaubert to a
married woman whose husband was absent and whose
name has come down to us—Eulalie Foucaud de Lenglade;
and with her, on a Saturday night, "in a bedroom like
mine, low-ceilinged, with a floor of red tiles, at this same
hour, for I have just heard it strike half past two," he
finally found the *volupté* whose delay he had been lament-
ing in the earlier pages of this *Intimate Notebook.* That
made a great difference. Little wonder that he refers to

the voyage as "my wonderful trip," keeps touching his linen suit hanging in the closet, and looks down on the "Good little children! Sweet young things!" at the ball in Rouen.

The travel notes here in the *Intimate Notebook* supplement the longer account, and their staccato touch resembles that of the famous notes of the 1849–50 trip to Egypt and the Near East. The longer account, which was doubtless meant to be read by his family, contains no reference whatever to *the* episode in Marseille, and even here, in the *Intimate Notebook,* in these "pages that I mean no one to read," he is careful.

A few details:

"old Moutna." Unidentifiable; perhaps a mistranscription.

"the Indies." Suggested by Jean Bruneau as a possible reading of Flaubert's hand. The French texts have the improbable *aux ports*—"at the ports."

"I practice medicine out of philanthropy" is followed in the transcript by *marché pour avoir*—puzzling, and omitted in the published French text.

"if the cock has crowed as in *Hamlet*" isn't quite clear —why "if"?

The final words, "farewell to another day," are followed in both French texts by a muddle: *candide, le sommeil viendrait, comme voilà une nuit bien employée, ô projets.* Probably an entry made at 4 A.M. was less legible to the transcriber than Flaubert's usual hand.

15. "Still the Orient." After getting his degree, Flaubert is nevertheless still living at home during the academic

year 1840–41. Following his father's wish, he was scheduled to enroll in the Law School in Paris at this time. Registration was postponed for a year: no one knows why.

He is suffering from travel fever following his "wonderful trip." (See also aphorism xxiv, below.) He will continue to long for the "Orient" until he sets out for it— i.e. for Egypt and the Near East—with Maxime du Camp in 1849, following his composition of the first version of *The Temptation of Saint Anthony.* That trip will be a kind of "purge of exoticism," and on his return he will begin his strenuous labors on *Madame Bovary.* In the meantime he will have traveled to Italy in 1845 on an ill-conceived and ill-fated excursion in which he and his parents accompanied his sister and her new husband on their honeymoon. Those, and a trip to Tunisia in 1858 to do research for *Salammbô,* will be Flaubert's only other major journeys.

"ABC." Apparently a travel guide. Unidentified.

16. "I don't believe it." Neither prediction was fulfilled. Jean Bruneau points out that like Flaubert himself, most of the principal male characters in his novels are non-dancers!

17. *"spettatore*—spectator." Dubious readings in both French texts.

18. "the Montyon prize." The *prix Montyon de Vertu.* Three or four of these prizes, amounting to about four hundred francs each, are awarded each June by the French Academy to poor citizens as rewards for virtuous

actions—devotion on the part of an old servant or a member of a family, acts of courage, etc. Funds for the purpose were bequeathed by the Baron de Montyon (1733–1820). There is also a Montyon literary prize, also awarded by the Academy.

19. "not because I love anyone." Cf. *November:* "I have offered bouquets of flowers to women I did not love, hoping that love would come that way, as I had heard it might. I have written letters addressed to any woman at random, to summon up my tears by writing—and they came. The slightest smile on a woman's lips made my heart melt deliciously—and then, that was all! So much happiness was not for me. Who could love me?"

20. "I would have to attach myself. . . ." This, too, is echoed in *November:* "I could see nothing to which I might attach myself, neither the world nor solitude, neither knowledge nor impiety nor religion; I wandered amid them all like a soul which hell rejects and heaven repulses."

21. "Chéruel." Both French texts have "Chevreuil," but Flaubert must be referring to the historian Pierre-Adolphe Chéruel, who had been his teacher at the *lycée* and had become his friend.

22. "there will be others spent in the _____." The last word of this entry is omitted in both French texts. Did Flaubert omit it from the manuscript? A possibility is *bordel.*

23. "one longs to be a woman." Cf. *November:* "I wished that I were a woman for her beauty, I wished that like her I might strip myself naked, let my hair fall to my heels, mirror and admire myself in the stream."

24. "not the slightest sense of rhythm." Here is Flaubert doing himself an injustice. He was soon to show in *November,* and, later, supremely in *Madame Bovary,* that he was a master of rhythm. Perhaps this lament reflects his age. Young people who worry profoundly about the limits of their intelligence, for example, are often the most intelligent of all. Remember, we have recently seen Flaubert walking around the Swiss Lake in Versailles with his former professor, Gourgaud, worrying about his literary vocation!

25. "I am writing these pages in order to reread them in a year, in thirty years." Did Flaubert ever reread this *Intimate Notebook?* We do not know. We only know that he never threw it away.

26. "Art is nothing but this strange translation of thought by form." As we have indicated in these notes, both parts of the *Intimate Notebook*—those written before and after the five-month break—contain many expressions of sentiment, and some details of fact, that are echoed in Flaubert's early Romantic novel *November*. The *Intimate Notebook* is thus a precious indication of the autobiographical nature of much of the material used in the construction of that novel, and of how and how much Flaubert transformed these autobiographical feelings and

events into fiction—for *November* is his first true, serious
fiction. By comparing various dates and references in
Flaubert's correspondence and elsewhere, Jean Bruneau
(*op. cit.*, pp. 311–12) has concluded that at the time of
the last entry in the *Intimate Notebook* (probably mid-
1841), *November*—which he calls "the masterpiece of
Flaubert's youth"—had already been begun. It is thus
easy to understand the abandoning of the *Intimate Notebook*. Art was taking over—art, "that strange translation
of thought by form."

Flaubert, perhaps rightly, did not publish *November*,
but it was issued posthumously and has been translated
into English and German and perhaps other languages.
The latest English-language edition is a re-issue of the
translation by Frank Jellinek (London, Michael Joseph,
1966; New York, Serendipity Press, 1967). For those in-
terested in the art of fiction, and in the early development
of great writers, it is moving to read the polished prose of
that heavily Romantic novel, remembering how much of
it was earlier set down in the fragmentary, passionate first
flights that make up this *Intimate Notebook*.

The year after the *Intimate Notebook* ends, 1842,
Gustave Flaubert finally enrolled in the Law School in
Paris, but after reading law for a time in a desultory and
disgusted way he fell victim to a series of epileptic or
pseudo-epileptic attacks that freed him from the necessity
of preparing to lead an "active" life. He returned to
Rouen and his family. Then came the sudden deaths of
his father and sister, and Gustave and his mother and
niece moved definitively to their country house at Crois-

set, on the Seine outside Rouen. There, except for the few intervals of travel already mentioned, and occasional winter residence in Paris, he devoted himself to his niece's education and, for the rest of his life, to the writing of his novels.

Gustave Flaubert

Intimate Notebook
1840-1841

Translated by Francis Steegmuller

"I go from hope to anxiety, from wild optimism, to dreary negation; it's rain and sun, but it's a gilded cardboard sun and a nasty rain with no storm." These words were written by one of France's greatest writers, the future author of *Madame Bovary*, when he was eighteen years old. At that time Gustave Flaubert was living with his parents in Rouen, dutifully following his father's wishes by studying to enter the Paris Law School. Fortunately, however, his true ambitions were distinctly literary, and it was to an ordinary schoolboy's copybook that Flaubert confided his earliest longings and most intimate thoughts.

In 1965 the text of this precious document was discovered in France, and published there for the first time. It was immediately greeted as an authentic and charmingly candid portrait of Flaubert experiencing the first tremors of his future creativity. In this journal he reveals himself to be a romantic, fiercely self-

(continued on back flap)